Published by Christian Focus Publications Ltd
Geanies House, Fearn, Tain, Ross-shire IV20 1TW www.christianfocus.com

Copyright © John Brown Brian Wright
ISBN: 978-1-5271-0946-9

This edition published in 2023
Cover illustration and internal illustrations by Lisa Flanagan
Cover and internal design by Lisa Flanagan
Printed and bound in China

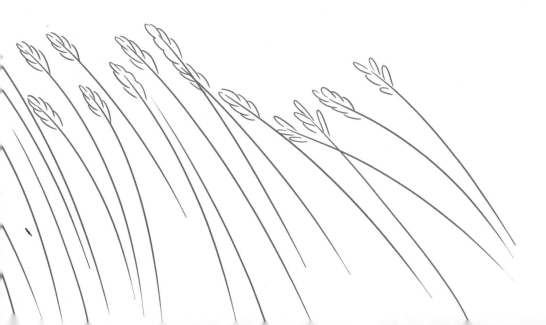

Joel

& the Locusts

John Brown
Brian Wright

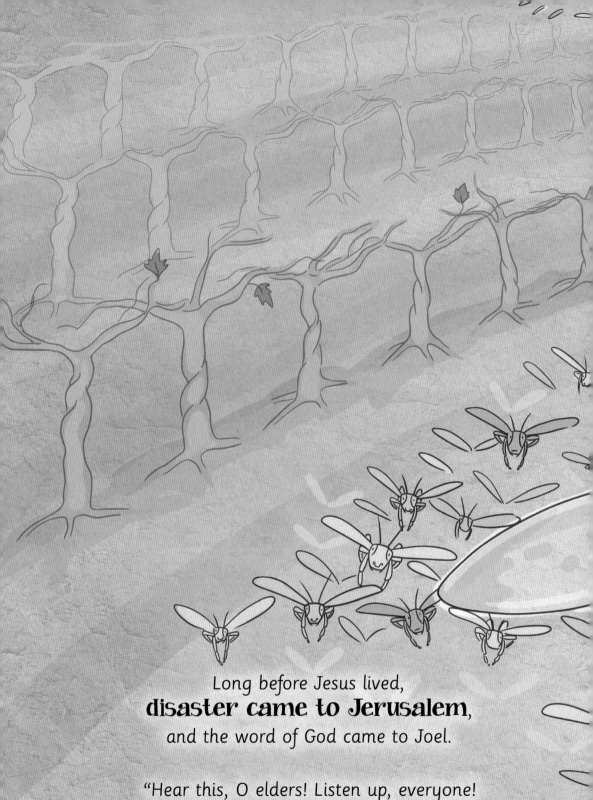

Long before Jesus lived,
disaster came to Jerusalem,
and the word of God came to Joel.

"Hear this, O elders! Listen up, everyone!
Something unheard of has happened that
you need to tell your children about!

"An army of locusts have **chomped** up our crops, **gobbled** down our grapes, **devoured** our vines, and **stripped** our trees bare!"

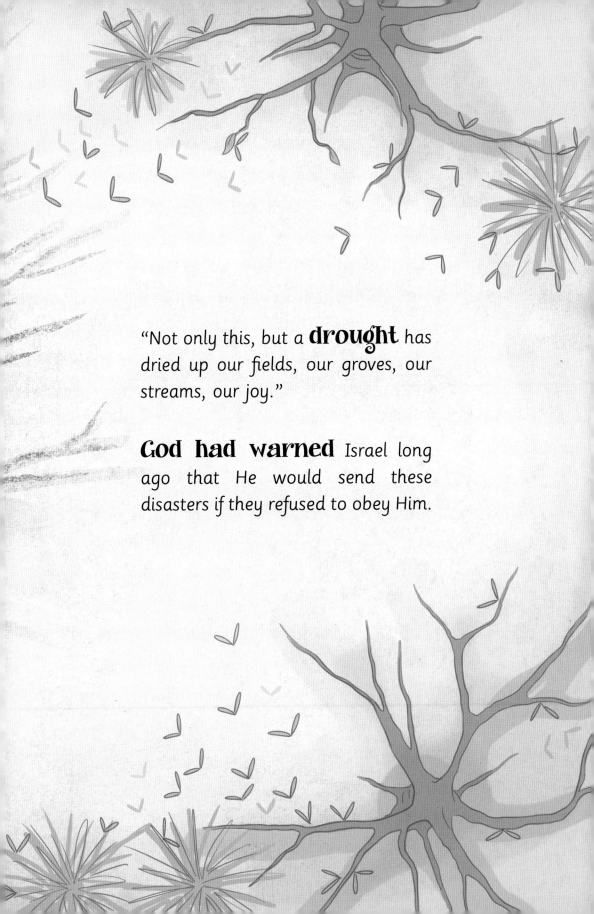

"Not only this, but a **drought** has dried up our fields, our groves, our streams, our joy."

God had warned Israel long ago that He would send these disasters if they refused to obey Him.

"Weep, newlyweds!

Mourn, priests!

Despair, farmers!

Grieve, grape growers! Wail, everyone!
For **everything is ruined!**"

"Put on sackcloth, you priests! Pray all night for forgiveness! Announce a fast! Assemble everyone at the temple to **cry out to God for mercy!**

"**The day of the Lord is near**, when God Almighty will destroy those who disobey Him!"

"Our **food** is gone, our **fields** are burnt, our **streams** are dry, our **cattle** wander, and our **sheep** suffer.

"I cry out to you, O Lord, and even the animals groan in longing for you! **Have mercy on us! Save us!**"

God heard Joel and told him of a day in the future, **"the day of the Lord,"** when He will come with His angelic army to set things right.

But setting things right means judging wicked people, so **everyone must repent** and call on God right now while there is still time!

"He will come with a large and mighty
army to retake His city."

"Great will be the day of the Lord!
Who can endure it?"

"Yet even now," says the Lord, "I will forgive you if you repent and return to Me with all your heart. **Don't just pretend to be sorry; prove it!"**

The Lord is gracious and compassionate, slow to anger and abounding in lovingkindness. He **forgives** those who truly repent.

"**Stop** everything!
Blow a trumpet!
Announce a fast!

Gather everyone, from the elders to nursing infants —
even the bride and groom about to be married!"

Let the priests weep and say,
"Have compassion on Your people, O Lord."

"Then **the Lord will forgive** His people and restore the rain and the grain, the grapes and the olive oil — everything the locusts ate and the drought dried up."

"God will drive out His people's enemies, and the land will be **free from fear** and **full of joy**, for the Lord has done great things."

You will have **plenty to eat** and **always be satisfied**, and you will praise the name of the Lord your God who has treated you so wonderfully.

You will know by these blessings that **I am with you**, and that **I am the Lord your God**; and that there is no other god; and that My people will never be put to shame.

"In those days,
I will pour out My Holy Spirit
on all My people — not just on judges like Samson and
kings like David — but on everyone — male and female,
old and young, slave and free."

"You will know when this happens because some will
prophesy, some will dream dreams,
and some will see visions."

"I will announce the day of the Lord with **signs for all to see**. The sun will turn dark, the moon will look blood-red, and there will be blood and fire and columns of smoke."

"In that day, **whoever calls upon the name of the Lord will be saved,** for He will spare those whom He chooses."

"I will gather all the nations of the earth to a place called the 'Valley of the Lord's Judgment.'"

"On that day the Lord will judge the nations,
render **His verdict**, and punish the wicked."

"But **the Lord is a refuge** for His people. 'Then you will know that I am the Lord your God who dwells in Jerusalem, making it **holy and safe forever**.'"

"In that day the mountains will **drip with wine**, the hills will **flow with milk**, the brooks will **gush with water**, and a spring from the Lord's house will water the Valley of Shittim.

"The Lord's people will **dwell in the Lord's land forever**, free from enemies, for the Lord dwells in Zion, which is Jerusalem."

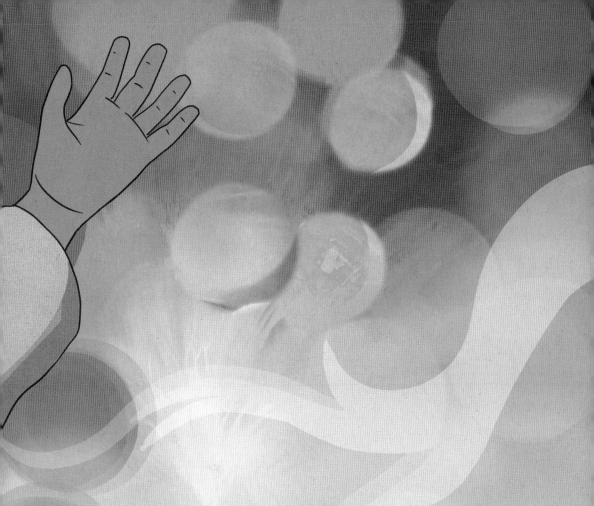

The Lord has come, just as God told Joel. He came as Jesus, and **whoever calls on the name of the Lord Jesus will be saved** and will receive the Holy Spirit just as God promised through Joel!

And **the Lord Jesus is coming back some day!** When He does, He will judge the wicked but forgive those who have repented and trusted in Him. Then He will restore the earth and live with His people forever and forever!

Christian Focus Publications publishes books for adults and children under its four main imprints: Christian Focus, CF4K, Mentor, and Christian Heritage. Our books reflect our conviction that God's Word is reliable and that Jesus is the way to know Him, and live for ever with Him.

Our children's publication list covers pre-school to early teens. We also publish personal and family devotionals, biographies and inspirational stories that children will love.

From pre-school board books to teenage apologetics, we have it covered!

Christian Focus Publications Ltd,
Geanies House, Fearn, Ross-shire,
IV20 1TW, Scotland,
United Kingdom.
www.christianfocus.com

CF4•K

*Because you're never
too young to know Jesus*